FIX IT QUICK™

APPETIZERS

Publications International, Ltd.

Favorite Brand Name Recipes at www.fbnr.com

Pictured on the front cover *(clockwise from top left):* Grilled Summer Bruschetta *(page 24),* BLT Dip *(page 6),* Tuna in Crispy Wonton Cups *(page 104)* and Mini Marinated Beef Skewers *(page 70).*
Pictured on the back cover: French-Style Pizza Bites *(page 78).*

ISBN-13: 978-1-4127-2730-3
ISBN-10: 1-4127-2730-8

Library of Congress Control Number: 2007933669

Manufactured in China.

8 7 6 5 4 3 2 1

Microwave Cooking: Microwave ovens vary in wattage. Use the cooking times as guidelines and check for doneness before adding more time.

Preparation/Cooking Times: Preparation times are based on the approximate amount of time required to assemble the recipe before cooking, baking, chilling or serving. These times include preparation steps such as measuring, chopping and mixing. The fact that some preparations and cooking can be done simultaneously is taken into account. Preparation of optional ingredients and serving suggestions is not included.

table of contents

zippy dips & spreads............... 4

easy finger foods 24

hearty snacks 54

fancy party noshes 84

crunchy munchies 108

acknowledgments 124

index 125

zippy dips &
spreads

apple salsa with cilantro and lime

1 cup diced unpeeled red apples
¼ cup diced red onion
¼ cup minced Anaheim chile pepper
½ jalapeño pepper, seeded and minced* (optional)
2 tablespoons lime juice
1 teaspoon chopped fresh cilantro
⅛ teaspoon salt
¼ teaspoon black pepper
Tortilla chips

Jalapeño peppers can sting and irritate the skin, so wear rubber gloves when handling peppers and do not touch your eyes.

1. Combine all ingredients except tortilla chips in large bowl; mix well. Cover with plastic wrap and refrigerate at least 30 minutes or overnight.

2. Serve with tortilla chips.   *Makes 2 cups*

apple salsa with cilantro and lime

blt dip

1 envelope LIPTON® RECIPE SECRETS® Onion Soup Mix*
1 container (8 ounces) sour cream
1 cup HELLMANN'S® or BEST FOODS® Real Mayonnaise
1 medium tomato, chopped (about 1 cup)
½ cup cooked crumbled bacon (about 6 slices) or bacon bits
Shredded lettuce

Also terrific with LIPTON® RECIPE SECRETS® Golden Onion Soup Mix.

1. In medium bowl, combine all ingredients except lettuce; chill, if desired.

2. Garnish with lettuce and serve with your favorite dippers.

Makes 3 cups dip

Prep Time: 10 minutes

easiest three-cheese fondue

1 tablespoon butter
¼ cup finely chopped onion
2 cloves garlic, minced
1 tablespoon all-purpose flour
¾ cup milk
2 cups (8 ounces) shredded mild or sharp Cheddar cheese
1 package (3 ounces) cream cheese, cut into cubes
½ cup (2 ounces) crumbled blue cheese
⅛ teaspoon ground red pepper
4 to 6 drops hot pepper sauce
Breadsticks and assorted fresh vegetables for dipping

1. Melt butter in small saucepan over medium heat. Add onion and garlic; cook and stir 2 to 3 minutes or until tender. Stir in flour; cook 2 minutes, stirring constantly.

2. Stir milk into saucepan; bring to a boil. Boil, stirring constantly, about 1 minute or until thickened. Reduce heat to low. Add cheeses; cook and stir until melted. Stir in red pepper and pepper sauce. Pour fondue into serving dish. Serve with dippers.

Makes about 8 servings

Prep and Cook Time: 20 minutes

blt dip

ortega® green chile guacamole

2 medium very ripe avocados, seeded, peeled and mashed
1 can (4 ounces) ORTEGA® Diced Green Chiles
2 large green onions, chopped
2 tablespoons olive oil
1 teaspoon lime juice
1 clove garlic, finely chopped
¼ teaspoon salt
  Tortilla chips

COMBINE avocados, chiles, green onions, olive oil, lime juice, garlic and salt in medium bowl. Cover; refrigerate for at least 1 hour. Serve with chips.

Makes 2 cups

quick & easy hummus

1 clove garlic, peeled
1 can (about 15 ounces) chickpeas, rinsed and drained
2 tablespoons torn fresh mint leaves (optional)
2 tablespoons olive oil
2 tablespoons lemon juice
2 teaspoons dark sesame oil
½ teaspoon salt
⅛ teaspoon ground red pepper *or* ¼ teaspoon hot pepper sauce

With motor running, drop garlic clove through feed tube of food processor. Add remaining ingredients to food processor. Cover; process until hummus is well combined and is desired consistency (the longer the hummus is processed the smoother the texture). *Makes 4 servings*

Serving Suggestion: Serve with vegetable dippers or pita wedges.

Tip: Leftover hummus may be covered and refrigerated up to 1 week. Hummus makes a great sandwich spread for pitas.

ortega® green chile guacamole

onion & white bean spread

1 can (about 15 ounces) cannellini or Great Northern
    beans, rinsed and drained
2 cloves garlic, minced
¼ cup minced green onions
¼ cup grated Parmesan cheese
¼ cup olive oil
1 tablespoon fresh rosemary leaves, finely chopped
  Additional olive oil
  French bread slices

1. Place all ingredients except additional olive oil and bread slices in food processor. Process 30 to 40 seconds or until mixture is almost smooth.

2. Spoon bean mixture into serving bowl. Drizzle additional olive oil over spread just before serving. Serve with bread slices.   *Makes 1¼ cups*

Tip: For a more rustic spread, place all ingredients in a medium bowl and mash with a potato masher.

hot artichoke dip

1 cup mayonnaise
1 cup sour cream
¼ cup grated Parmesan cheese
¼ cup chopped roasted red peppers
1 can (14 ounces) artichoke hearts, drained and chopped
1⅓ cups *French's*® French Fried Onions, divided
  Assorted crackers or bagel chips

1. Preheat oven to 375°F. Combine mayonnaise, sour cream, cheese, roasted peppers, artichokes and ⅔ *cup* French Fried Onions. Spoon into 9-inch pie plate or 1-quart shallow baking dish.

2. Bake 25 minutes or until hot. Top with remaining onions and bake 5 minutes or until onions are golden. Serve with assorted crackers or bagel chips.   *Makes 3 cups*

Prep Time: 10 minutes
Cook Time: 30 minutes

onion & white bean spread

texas pecan and beef dip

  1 tablespoon vegetable oil
½ cup pecan pieces
  3 tablespoons thinly sliced green onions
  1 package (8 ounces) cream cheese, softened and cut into cubes
⅓ cup lager beer
½ (2.2-ounce) jar dried beef, rinsed in hot water, drained and cut
      into ¼-inch pieces
1½ teaspoons BBQ seasoning blend
    Breadsticks, pita bread or assorted fresh vegetables for dipping

1. Heat oil in small saucepan over medium heat. Add pecans and onions; cook and stir 3 to 5 minutes or until pecans are toasted and onions are tender.

2. Add cream cheese and beer to saucepan; cook over medium-low heat until cheese is melted. Stir in dried beef and BBQ seasoning; cook and stir until hot. Serve with breadsticks.   *Makes 1½ cups dip*

Prep and Cook Time: 18 minutes

olive & feta dip

  1 cup HELLMANN'S® or BEST FOODS® Real Mayonnaise
  4 ounces cream cheese, softened
  3 ounces feta cheese, crumbled
⅓ cup chopped kalamata olives
  3 green onions, chopped
  1 clove garlic, pressed or finely chopped
¼ teaspoon dried oregano leaves, crushed

1. Preheat oven to 350°F.

2. In medium bowl, combine all ingredients. Spoon into 1½-quart casserole Bake 30 minutes or until heated through. Serve with pita wedges or your favorite dippers.   *Makes 2 cups dip*

Prep Time: 10 Minutes
Cook Time: 30 Minutes

texas pecan and beef dip

chili dip

1 container (16 ounces) sour cream
1 medium tomato, chopped (about 1 cup)
1 can (4 ounces) chopped green chilies, drained
1 package KNORR® Leek recipe mix
3 to 4 teaspoons chili powder

- In medium bowl, combine all ingredients; chill at least 2 hours.

- Stir before serving. Serve with corn chips or cut-up vegetables.

Makes about 3 cups dip

Cheese Chili Dip: Stir in 1 cup shredded Monterey Jack cheese (about 4 ounces).

Prep Time: 5 minutes
Chill Time: 2 hours

spicy turkey ham spread

1 pound turkey ham, cut into chunks
¼ cup chopped onion
¼ cup Dijon mustard
4 teaspoons Worcestershire sauce
¼ teaspoon ground red pepper

1. In food processor bowl fitted with metal blade, process ham, onion, mustard, Worcestershire sauce and ground red pepper until smooth. Cover and chill.

2. To serve, spoon mixture into red or green bell pepper halves, accompanied with melba toast rounds, if desired. *Makes 2 cups*

Additional Ingredients: Two large red and green peppers, cut in half and seeded. As needed, Melba toast rounds or assorted crackers.

Favorite recipe from **National Turkey Federation**

hot crab-cheddar spread

1 (8-ounce) container crabmeat, drained and shredded
8 ounces CABOT® Mild or Sharp Cheddar, grated (about 2 cups)
½ cup mayonnaise
¼ teaspoon Worcestershire sauce

1. Preheat oven to 350°F.

2. In medium bowl, mix together all ingredients thoroughly. Transfer to small (1-quart) baking dish. Bake for 25 to 35 minutes, or until lightly browned on top and bubbling at edges. Serve with crackers or bread toasts.

Makes 8 to 10 servings

chipotle chile-sour cream dip

3 to 4 canned chipotle chiles in adobo sauce
½ cup mayonnaise
1 cup sour cream
½ package (8 ounces) cream cheese
1 teaspoon lime juice
½ teaspoon salt
2 green onions, finely chopped
　Tortilla chips or raw vegetables for dipping

Process chiles and mayonnaise in blender or food processor until smooth. Add sour cream, cream cheese, lime juice and salt; process until combined. Transfer dip to serving dish; sprinkle with chopped green onions. Cover and chill until ready to serve. Serve with chips or vegetables.

Makes about 2 cups

Note: Dip can be prepared up to five days in advance. Refrigerate. Top with green onions just before serving.

nutty bacon cheeseball

1 package (8 ounces) cream cheese, softened
½ cup milk
2 cups (8 ounces) shredded sharp Cheddar cheese
2 cups (8 ounces) shredded Monterey Jack cheese
¼ cup (1 ounce) crumbled blue cheese
10 slices bacon, cooked, crumbled and divided
¾ cup finely chopped pecans, divided
¼ cup finely minced green onions (white parts only)
1 jar (2 ounces) diced pimiento, drained
Salt and black pepper
¼ cup minced fresh parsley
1 tablespoon poppy seeds

1. Beat cream cheese and milk in large bowl with electric mixer at low speed until blended. Add cheeses. Beat at medium speed until well mixed. Add half of bacon, half of pecans, green onions and pimiento. Beat at medium speed until well mixed. Add salt and pepper to taste. Divide mixture in half. Shape each half into ball; wrap tightly in plastic wrap. Refrigerate at least 2 hours or until chilled.

2. Combine remaining bacon, pecans, parsley and poppy seeds in pie plate. Unwrap balls; roll each cheeseball in bacon mixture. Wrap tightly in plastic wrap; refrigerate up to 24 hours. *Makes about 24 servings*

mediterranean dip

1 envelope LIPTON® RECIPE SECRETS® Vegetable Soup Mix
1 container (16 ounces) sour cream
½ cup seeded and diced cucumber
4 ounces feta or blue cheese, crumbled
2 tablespoons chopped red onion
½ teaspoon dried oregano leaves (optional)

In medium bowl, combine all ingredients; chill at least 2 hours. Serve with assorted fresh vegetables, pita bread triangles, bread sticks or skewered cooked beef or chicken. *Makes 2½ cups*

nutty bacon cheeseball

fast guacamole and "chips"

 2 ripe avocados
½ cup chunky salsa
¼ teaspoon hot pepper sauce (optional)
½ seedless cucumber, sliced into ⅛-inch-thick rounds

1. Cut avocados in half; remove and discard pits. Scoop flesh into medium bowl; mash with fork.

2. Stir in salsa and hot pepper sauce, if desired. Transfer guacamole to serving bowl. Serve with cucumber "chips."   *Makes 8 servings*

tex-mex artichoke dip

 1 cup *French's® Gourmayo™* Smoked Chipotle Light Mayonnaise
½ cup sour cream
 1 can (14 ounces) artichoke hearts, drained well and chopped
¾ cup shredded Monterey Jack cheese
¼ cup chopped roasted red pepper
 2 green onions, chopped

1. Preheat oven to 375°F. In large bowl, combine mayonnaise and sour cream. Stir in artichokes, cheese, red pepper and green onions. Spoon into 9-inch pie plate or 1-quart shallow baking dish.

2. Bake for 30 minutes or until hot. Stir well before serving. Serve with assorted crackers and cut-up vegetables.   *Makes about 12 servings*

Prep Time: 10 minutes
Cook Time: 30 minutes

fast guacamole and "chips"

fiesta dip

1 package (1 ounce) LAWRY'S® Taco Spices & Seasonings
1 container (16 ounces) sour cream
   Tortilla chips and assorted crisp vegetables

In medium bowl, combine Taco Spices & Seasonings and sour cream. Cover and refrigerate for about 1 hour. Serve with chips.   *Makes 2 cups*

Variation: Use as a flavorful spread for flour tortillas when making wraps.

Prep Time: 3 minutes
Chill Time: 1 hour

pineapple-mango salsa

1½ cups fresh DOLE® Tropical Gold® Pineapple, cut into chunks
   1 ripe DOLE® Mango, peeled and chopped
   ½ cup chopped red cabbage
   ⅓ cup finely chopped DOLE® Red Onion
   ¼ cup chopped fresh cilantro
   2 tablespoons lime juice
   1 to 2 serrano or jalapeño chiles, seeded and minced

• Stir together pineapple chunks, mango, cabbage, red onion, cilantro, lime juice and chiles in medium bowl. Cover and chill for at least 30 minutes to blend flavors. Serve salsa over grilled chicken with grilled vegetables. Garnish with lime wedges, if desired.   *Makes 3½ cups*

Variation: Salsa can also be served as a dip with tortilla chips or spooned over quesadillas or tacos.

Prep Time: 15 minutes
Chill Time: 30 minutes

fiesta dip

olive tapenade

　1 can (16 ounces) medium pitted black olives
　½ cup pimiento-stuffed green olives
　1 tablespoon roasted garlic*
　½ teaspoon dry mustard
　½ cup (2 ounces) crumbled feta cheese
　1 tablespoon olive oil
　　Toasted bread slices

To roast garlic, preheat oven to 400°F. Remove outer layers of papery skin and cut ¼ inch off top of garlic head. Place cut side up on a piece of heavy-duty foil. Drizzle with 2 teaspoons olive oil; wrap tightly in foil. Bake 25 to 30 minutes or until cloves feel soft when pressed. Cool slightly before squeezing out garlic pulp.

1. Process olives, roasted garlic and mustard in food processor or blender until finely chopped.

2. Combine olive mixture, feta cheese and oil in medium bowl; stir until well blended. Serve with bread. *Makes 1¾ cups dip*

Tip: For the best flavor, prepare this tapenade several hours or one day ahead to allow the flavors to blend.

reuben dip

　1 cup HELLMANN'S® or BEST FOODS® Real Mayonnaise
　1 cup sour cream
　1 cup grated Swiss cheese (about 4 ounces)
　½ cup sauerkraut, drained
　4 ounces lean pastrami or corned beef, chopped
　¼ cup ketchup

1. Preheat oven to 350°F.

2. In 1½-quart baking dish, combine all ingredients. Bake 30 minutes or until heated through. Serve, if desired, with toasted pumpernickel or party-size rye bread. *Makes 3⅓ cups dip*

Prep Time: 5 minutes
Cook Time: 30 minutes

olive tapenade

easy finger foods

grilled summer bruschetta

¾ cup WISH-BONE® 5 Cheese Italian Dressing
2 medium red, orange and/or yellow bell peppers, quartered
2 medium yellow squash and/or green zucchini, quartered lengthwise
1 tablespoon chopped fresh basil leaves
1 loaf Italian or French bread (about 15-inches long), cut ½-inch slices

1. In large shallow nonaluminum baking dish or plastic bag, pour ¼ cup Wish-Bone 5 Cheese Italian Dressing over red peppers and squash; turn to coat. Cover, or close bag, and marinate in refrigerator 15 minutes.

2. Meanwhile, brush bread with ¼ cup Dressing and grill or broil until golden. Remove vegetables from marinade, reserving marinade. Grill or broil vegetables, turning once and brushing with reserved marinade, 15 minutes or until vegetables are tender. Cool vegetables slightly, then coarsely chop.

3. In medium bowl, combine remaining ¼ cup Dressing, basil and, if desired, salt and ground black pepper to taste. Stir in vegetables and toss to coat. To serve, spoon vegetable mixture on toasted bread.   *Makes 30 appetizers*

Prep Time: 15 minutes
Marinate Time: 15 minutes
Cook Time: 20 minutes

grilled summer bruschetta

mini chickpea cakes

1 can (about 15 ounces) chickpeas, rinsed and drained
1 cup shredded carrots
⅓ cup seasoned dry bread crumbs
¼ cup creamy Italian salad dressing
1 egg
Additional creamy Italian salad dressing

1. Preheat oven to 375°F. Spray baking sheets with nonstick cooking spray.

2. Mash chickpeas coarsely in medium bowl with potato masher. Stir in carrots, bread crumbs, salad dressing and egg; mix well.

3. Shape chickpea mixture into small patties, using about 1 tablespoon mixture for each. Place on prepared baking sheets.

4. Bake 15 to 18 minutes or until chickpea cakes are lightly browned on both sides, turning halfway through baking time. Serve warm with additional salad dressing for dipping. *Makes about 2 dozen cakes*

summer fruits
with peanut butter-honey dip

⅓ cup peanut butter
2 tablespoons milk
2 tablespoons honey
1 tablespoon apple juice or water
⅛ teaspoon ground cinnamon
2 cups melon balls, including cantaloupe and honeydew
1 peach or nectarine, pitted and cut into 8 wedges
1 banana, peeled and thickly sliced

1. Place peanut butter in small bowl; gradually stir in milk and honey until blended. Stir in apple juice and cinnamon until mixture is smooth.

2. Serve dip with prepared fruits. *Makes 4 servings (about ½ cup dip)*

Prep Time: 20 minutes

mini chickpea cakes

chile 'n' cheese spirals

4 ounces cream cheese, softened
1 cup (4 ounces) shredded cheddar cheese
1 can (4 ounces) ORTEGA® Diced Green Chiles
3 green onions, sliced
½ cup chopped red bell pepper
1 can (2.25 ounces) chopped ripe olives
4 (8-inch) taco-size flour tortillas
ORTEGA Salsa, any variety

COMBINE cream cheese, cheddar cheese, chiles, green onions, pepper and olives in medium bowl.

SPREAD ½ cup cheese mixture on each tortilla; roll up. Wrap each roll in plastic wrap; chill for 1 hour.

REMOVE plastic wrap; slice each roll into six ¾-inch pieces. Serve with salsa for dipping.   *Makes 24 appetizers*

Tip: Chile 'n' Cheese Spirals can be prepared and kept in the refrigerator for 1 to 2 days.

fast pesto focaccia

1 can (13.8 ounces) refrigerated pizza dough
2 tablespoons prepared pesto
4 sun-dried tomatoes, packed in oil, drained

1. Preheat oven to 425°F. Lightly grease 8-inch square baking pan. Unroll pizza dough. Fold in half; press gently into pan.

2. Spread pesto evenly over dough. Chop tomatoes or snip with kitchen scissors; sprinkle over pesto. Press tomatoes into dough. Using wooden spoon handle, make indentations in dough every 2 inches.

3. Bake 10 to 12 minutes or until golden brown. Cut into 16 squares. Serve warm or at room temperature.   *Makes 16 servings*

Prep and Cook Time: 20 minutes

chile 'n' cheese spirals

tomato and caper crostini

16 slices French bread
4 plum tomatoes, finely chopped
3 tablespoons capers, drained
2 teaspoons dried basil
1 tablespoon extra-virgin olive oil
½ cup (2 ounces) crumbled feta cheese with sun-dried tomatoes and basil or any variety

1. Preheat oven to 350°F.

2. Place bread slices on ungreased baking sheet in single layer. Bake 15 minutes or just until golden brown. Cool completely.

3. Meanwhile, combine tomatoes, capers, basil and oil in small bowl; mix well.

4. Just before serving, spoon tomato mixture on each bread slice; sprinkle with cheese.   *Makes 16 crostini*

quick tip

Crostini refers to small thin slices of bread drizzled with olive oil and toasted. It also refers to an appetizer with various toppings. Make extra toasts to keep on hand for a variety of appetizers. Serve with spreads and dips or use as a base for other crostini toppings.

tomato and caper crostini

sausage-stuffed mushrooms

4 ounces uncooked turkey Italian sausage, casings removed
2 tablespoons plain dry bread crumbs
4 medium portobello mushroom caps
1 tablespoon olive oil
¼ cup shredded Asiago cheese

1. Preheat toaster oven to 325°F. Crumble sausage into small skillet. Cook over medium-high heat until no longer pink; drain fat. Remove from heat; stir in bread crumbs.

2. Brush both sides of mushroom caps lightly with oil. Spoon sausage mixture evenly into mushroom caps.

3. Place mushrooms, stuffing side up, on toaster oven tray. Sprinkle 1 tablespoon cheese over each mushroom. Bake 15 minutes or until cheese melts and mushrooms are tender.   *Makes 4 servings*

bubbling wisconsin cheese bread

½ cup (2 ounces) shredded Wisconsin Mozzarella cheese
⅓ cup mayonnaise or salad dressing
⅛ teaspoon garlic powder
⅛ teaspoon onion powder
 1 loaf (16 ounces) French bread, halved lengthwise
⅓ cup (1 ounce) grated Wisconsin Parmesan cheese

Preheat oven to 350°F. Combine mozzarella cheese, mayonnaise, garlic powder and onion powder in mixing bowl; mix well (mixture will be very thick). Spread half the mixture over each bread half. Sprinkle half the Parmesan cheese over each half. Bake 20 to 25 minutes or until bubbly and lightly browned.* Cut each half into 8 slices.   *Makes 16 servings*

To broil, position on rack 4 inches from heat for 3 to 5 minutes.

Favorite recipe from **Wisconsin Milk Marketing Board**

sausage-stuffed mushrooms

polenta pizzas

1 teaspoon olive oil
½ cup chopped onion
¼ pound bulk mild Italian sausage
1 can (8 ounces) pizza sauce
1 roll (16 ounces) prepared polenta
1 cup (4 ounces) shredded mozzarella

1. Preheat oven to 350°F. Spray 13×9-inch baking pan with nonstick cooking spray; set aside.

2. Heat oil in small skillet over medium heat. Add onion; cook and stir 3 minutes or until tender. Add sausage to skillet and brown 5 minutes, stirring to break up meat. Stir in pizza sauce; simmer 5 minutes.

3. Cut polenta roll into 16 slices; arrange in prepared pan. Spoon 1 heaping tablespoon sausage mixture over each polenta slice. Sprinkle 1 tablespoon cheese over each slice. Bake 15 minutes or until polenta is hot and cheese is melted. *Makes 4 to 6 servings*

roast beef roll-ups

1 package (8 ounces) cream cheese, softened
1 cup (4 ounces) crumbled blue cheese
1 teaspoon Dijon mustard
½ teaspoon black pepper
1 pound sliced deli roast beef
1 small red onion, thinly sliced
12 butter lettuce leaves (about 1 head)

1. Mix cream cheese, blue cheese, mustard and pepper in a small bowl until well blended. Spread each slice of roast beef with 1 tablespoon cheese mixture. Top with 1 to 2 slices onion and one leaf lettuce. Roll up beef slices starting at short end; secure with toothpick, if necessary.

2. Arrange rolls on serving platter. *Makes about 12 servings*

polenta pizzas

chili puffs

1 package (about 17 ounces) frozen puff pastry sheets, thawed
1 can (15 ounces) chili without beans
½ (8-ounce) package cream cheese, softened
½ cup (2 ounces) finely shredded sharp Cheddar cheese
   Sliced green onions (optional)

1. Preheat oven to 400°F.

2. Roll each sheet of puff pastry into 18×9-inch rectangle on lightly floured surface. Cut each rectangle into 18 (3-inch) squares. Press dough into 36 mini (1¾-inch) muffin cups. Bake 10 minutes.

3. Combine chili and cream cheese in medium bowl until smooth. Fill each pastry shell with 2 teaspoons chili mixture, pressing down centers of pastry to fill, if necessary. Sprinkle evenly with cheese.

4. Bake additional 5 to 7 minutes or until cheese is melted and edges of pastry are golden brown. Let stand in pan 5 minutes. Remove from pan. Garnish with onions. *Makes 36 puffs*

Tip: Use a pizza cutter to easily cut puff pastry sheets.

tortellini kabobs with pesto ranch dip

½ (16-ounce) bag frozen tortellini
1¼ cups prepared ranch salad dressing
½ cup grated Parmesan cheese
3 cloves garlic, minced
2 teaspoons dried basil

1. Cook tortellini according to package directions. Rinse and drain under cold water. Thread tortellini onto bamboo skewers, 2 tortellini per skewer.

2. Combine salad dressing, cheese, garlic and basil in small bowl. Serve tortellini kabobs with dip. *Makes 6 to 8 servings*

Prep and Cook Time: 30 minutes

chili puffs

honey roasted ham biscuits

1 (10-ounce) can refrigerated buttermilk biscuits
2 cups (12 ounces) diced HORMEL® CURE 81® ham
½ cup honey mustard
¼ cup finely chopped honey roasted peanuts, divided

Heat oven to 400°F. Separate biscuits. Place in muffin pan cups, pressing gently into bottoms and up sides of cups. In bowl, combine ham, honey mustard and 2 tablespoons peanuts. Spoon ham mixture evenly into biscuit cups. Sprinkle with remaining 2 tablespoons peanuts. Bake 15 to 17 minutes.

Makes 10 servings

ortega® nachos

1 can (16 ounces) ORTEGA® Refried Beans, heated
4 cups (4 ounces) tortilla chips
1½ cups (6 ounces) shredded Monterey Jack cheese
¼ cup ORTEGA Sliced Jalapeños
ORTEGA Salsa, any variety, sliced green onions, guacamole, sliced olives, chopped cilantro and sour cream (optional)

PREHEAT broiler.

SPREAD beans over bottom of large ovenproof platter or 15×10×1-inch jellyroll pan. Arrange chips over beans. Top with cheese and jalapeños.

BROIL for 1 to 1½ minutes or until cheese is melted. Top with salsa, green onions and other garnishes, if desired.

Makes 4 to 6 servings

honey roasted ham biscuits

tuna artichoke cups

1 can (6 ounces) tuna packed in water, drained, liquid reserved
¼ cup minced shallots
1 tablespoon white wine vinegar
¼ teaspoon ground coriander
½ (8-ounce) package cream cheese
1 can (14 ounces) artichoke hearts, drained and coarsely chopped
1 tablespoon lemon juice
½ teaspoon salt
¼ teaspoon white pepper
   Dash ground nutmeg
12 wonton wrappers
2 tablespoons butter, melted
   Chopped fresh parsley or chives (optional)

1. Preheat oven to 350°F.

2. Heat reserved tuna liquid, shallots, vinegar and coriander in small saucepan over medium-high heat. Bring to a boil. Reduce heat; simmer, uncovered, until liquid has evaporated. Add tuna and cream cheese; cook, stirring constantly, until cheese melts. Stir in artichokes, lemon juice, salt, pepper and nutmeg. Cool slightly.

3. Gently press 1 wonton wrapper into 12 standard (2½-inch) muffin cups, allowing ends to extend above edges of cups. Spoon tuna mixture evenly into wonton wrappers.

4. Brush edges of wonton wrappers with melted butter. Bake for 20 minutes or until tuna mixture is set and edges of wonton wrappers are browned. Garnish with parsley. *Makes 12 appetizers*

two tomato-kalamata crostini

    4 ounces baguette bread, cut into 20 (¼-inch-thick) slices
    5 ounces grape tomatoes, finely chopped
    8 sun-dried tomatoes, finely chopped (see tip)
   12 kalamata olives, pitted and finely chopped
    2 teaspoons cider vinegar
  1½ teaspoons dried basil
    1 teaspoon extra-virgin olive oil
   ⅛ teaspoon salt
    1 clove garlic, halved crosswise

1. Preheat oven to 350°F.

2. Place bread slices on large baking sheet. Bake 10 minutes or until golden brown around edges. Remove to wire racks; cool.

3. Combine grape tomatoes, sun-dried tomatoes, olives, vinegar, basil, oil and salt in small bowl. Toss thoroughly.

4. Rub bread slices with garlic. Top each bread slice with 1 tablespoon tomato mixture.

Makes 20 crostini

quick tip

You can purchase sun-dried tomatoes either packed in oil in jars or packaged dry in cellophane. The oil-packed variety tends to be more expensive but benefits from being soaked in liquid, making them ready to use. The dry variety needs to be rehydrated in liquid before using in this recipe. Follow the package directions to rehydrate.

stromboli sticks

1 package (13.8 ounces) refrigerated pizza crust dough
10 mozzarella cheese sticks
30 thin slices pepperoni
1 jar (1 pound 10 ounces) RAGÚ® Old World Style® Pasta Sauce, heated

1. Preheat oven to 425°F. Grease baking sheet; set aside.

2. Roll pizza dough into 13×10-inch rectangle. Cut in half crosswise, then cut each half into 5 strips.

3. Place 1 cheese stick on each strip of pizza dough, then top with 3 slices pepperoni. Fold edges over, sealing tightly.

4. Arrange Stromboli Sticks on prepared baking sheet, seam side down. Bake 15 minutes or until golden. Serve with Pasta Sauce, heated, for dipping.

Makes 10 sticks

Prep Time: 15 minutes
Cook Time: 15 minutes

cajun deviled eggs

6 hard-cooked eggs, peeled
3 tablespoons mayonnaise
½ teaspoon Cajun or Creole seasoning, divided
2 tablespoons finely chopped fresh parsley

1. Slice eggs in half lengthwise. Place yolks in small bowl. Add mayonnaise and Cajun seasoning; mix well. Pipe or spoon filling into egg whites. Cover and chill at least 30 minutes or up to 24 hours before serving.

2. Sprinkle with parsley before serving.   *Makes 12 servings*

stromboli sticks

tuscan white bean crostini

2 cans (about 15 ounces each) Great Northern or cannellini beans, rinsed and drained

½ large red bell pepper, finely chopped *or* ⅓ cup finely chopped roasted red bell pepper

⅓ cup finely chopped onion

⅓ cup red wine vinegar

3 tablespoons chopped fresh parsley

1 tablespoon olive oil

2 cloves garlic, minced

½ teaspoon dried oregano

¼ teaspoon black pepper

18 slices French bread, about ¼ inch thick

1. Combine beans, bell pepper and onion in large bowl.

2. Whisk together vinegar, parsley, oil, garlic, oregano and black pepper in small bowl. Pour over bean mixture; toss to coat. Cover; refrigerate 2 hours or overnight.

3. Prehet broiler. Arrange bread slices in single layer on large ungreased baking sheet or broiler pan. Broil, 6 to 8 inches from heat, 30 to 45 seconds or until bread slices are lightly toasted. Cool completely.

4. Top each toasted bread slice with about 3 tablespoons bean mixture.

Makes 18 crostini

tuscan white bean crostini

triangle tostadas

2 large (burrito size) flour tortillas
Vegetable oil
1 package (about 1 pound) lean ground pork
1 package (1 ounce) LAWRY'S® Taco Spices & Seasonings
⅔ cup water
1 can (16 ounces) refried beans, warmed

Toppings
Shredded lettuce and cheese, chopped tomatoes

Preheat oven to 400°F. Cut each tortilla into quarters, forming 4 triangles. Place triangles in single layer on baking sheet. Brush each side of triangle lightly with oil. Bake for 4 to 5 minutes or until golden brown and crispy; let cool. Meanwhile, in large skillet, brown ground pork over medium high heat until crumbly; drain fat. Stir in Taco Spices & Seasonings and water. Bring to a boil; reduce heat to low and cook, uncovered for 7 minutes or until pork is thoroughly cooked, stirring occasionally. To assemble tostadas, evenly divide and spread refried beans on each tortilla triangle. Spread about ¼ cup seasoned pork on top of beans. Top with shredded lettuce, cheese and tomatoes, as desired. *Makes 8 tostadas*

Variations: Cut each tortilla into 8 pieces and make mini appetizer tostadas. For additional toppings, try sliced black olives, sour cream, guacamole, salsa or jalapenos.

Prep Time: 15 minutes
Cook Time: 16 to 18 minutes

triangle tostada

artichoke crostini

1 jar (about 6 ounces) marinated artichoke hearts, drained and chopped
3 green onions, chopped
5 tablespoons grated Parmesan cheese, divided
2 tablespoons mayonnaise
12 slices French bread (½ inch thick)

1. Preheat broiler. Combine artichokes, green onions, 3 tablespoons cheese and mayonnaise in small bowl; mix well. Set aside.

2. Arrange bread slices on baking sheet. Broil 4 to 5 inches from heat 2 to 3 minutes on each side or until lightly browned.

3. Spread about 1 tablespoon artichoke mixture onto each bread slice; sprinkle with remaining 2 tablespoons cheese. Broil 1 to 2 minutes or until cheese is melted and lightly browned. Garnish with chopped red bell pepper.

Makes 12 crostini

Prep and Cook Time: 15 minutes

herb cheese twists

2 tablespoons butter or margarine
¼ cup grated Parmesan cheese
1 teaspoon dried parsley flakes
1 teaspoon dried basil
1 can (about 6 ounces) refrigerated buttermilk biscuits (5 count)

1. Preheat oven to 400°F. Lightly grease baking sheet. Microwave butter in small bowl on MEDIUM (50%) just until melted; cool slightly. Stir in cheese, parsley and basil. Set aside.

2. Pat each biscuit into 5×2-inch rectangle. Spread 1 teaspoon butter mixture onto each rectangle; cut each in half lengthwise. Twist each strip 3 or 4 times. Place on prepared baking sheet. Bake 8 to 10 minutes or until golden brown.

Makes 10 twists

Variation: Use ready-to-bake breadsticks. Spread the butter mixture onto the breadsticks, then bake them according to the package directions.

Prep and Cook Time: 20 minutes

artichoke crostini

sausage-bacon-apricot kabobs

1 package BOB EVANS® Italian Grillin' Sausage (approximately 5 links)
1 cup dried apricot halves
8 slices bacon
3 tablespoons apricot preserves
3 tablespoons lemon juice
1 tablespoon Dijon mustard
1 teaspoon Worcestershire sauce

Precook sausage 10 minutes in gently boiling water. Drain and cut into ¾-inch slices. Alternate sausage and apricots on 8 wooden skewers,* weaving bacon back and forth in ribbonlike fashion between them. Grill or broil over medium-high heat 3 to 4 minutes on each side. Combine preserves, lemon juice, mustard and Worcestershire in small bowl. Brush preserves mixture on kabobs; continue grilling, turning and basting frequently, until bacon is cooked through. Refrigerate leftovers.   *Makes 8 kabobs*

Soak wooden skewers in water 30 minutes before using to prevent burning.

quick tip

There are many types of skewers made specifically for broiling and grilling kabobs. Many cooks prefer to use bamboo skewers because the wood remains cool during serving. New metal and wood flat skewers have recently become popular because the food does not slip around when turning.

sausage-bacon-apricot kabobs

spanish tapas potatoes

Roasted Potatoes

2½ pounds small red potatoes, quartered

2 tablespoons olive oil

1 teaspoon coarse or kosher salt

½ teaspoon dried rosemary

Brava Sauce

1 can (about 14 ounces) diced tomatoes

⅓ cup olive oil

2 tablespoons red wine vinegar

1 tablespoon minced garlic

1 tablespoon chili powder

1 tablespoon paprika

¼ teaspoon salt

¼ teaspoon ground chipotle pepper

⅛ to ¼ teaspoon ground red pepper

1. Preheat oven to 425°F.

2. For potatoes, combine potatoes, 2 tablespoons oil, 1 teaspoon salt and rosemary in large bowl; toss to coat. Spread mixture on large baking sheet. Roast potatoes 35 to 40 minutes or until crisp and brown, turning every 10 minutes.

3. For sauce, combine tomatoes, ⅓ cup olive oil, vinegar, garlic, chili powder, paprika, ¼ teaspoon salt, chipotle pepper and red pepper in blender or food processor. Cover; process just until blended. Transfer to large saucepan. Cover; cook 5 minutes over medium-high heat until slightly thickened. Let stand until cooled.

4. To serve, drizzle sauce over potatoes or serve sauce in separate bowl for dipping. *Makes 10 to 12 appetizer servings*

Note: Sauce can be made up to 24 hours ahead of time. Cover and refrigerate. Bring to room temperature or reheat before serving.

spanish tapas potatoes

hearty
snacks

margherita panini bites

1 loaf (16 ounces) ciabatta or crusty Italian bread, cut into
  16 (½-inch) slices
8 teaspoons prepared pesto
16 fresh basil leaves
8 slices mozzarella cheese
24 thin slices plum tomatoes (about 2 to 4 tomatoes)
  Olive oil

1. Preheat indoor grill. Spread each of 8 slices bread with 1 teaspoon pesto. Top each slice with 2 basil leaves, 1 slice mozzarella cheese and 3 slices tomatoes. Top with remaining bread slices.

2. Brush both sides of sandwiches lightly with olive oil. Grill sandwiches 5 minutes or until lightly browned and cheese is melted.

3. Cut each sandwich into 4 pieces. Serve warm.   *Makes 32 panini bites*

margherita panini bites

beefy pinwheels

    1 package (8 ounces) cream cheese
    ¼ cup chopped pimiento-stuffed green olives
    2 tablespoons horseradish mustard
    6 (6- to 7-inch) flour tortillas
   12 small slices deli roast beef
    6 green onions, tops included

1. Place unwrapped cream cheese on paper plate. Microwave on HIGH 15 seconds or until softened.

2. Combine cream cheese, olives and mustard in small bowl; mix well.

3. Spread about 2 tablespoons cream cheese mixture over each tortilla. Top each with 2 overlapping slices of beef.

4. Place one onion on edge of tortilla, trimming to fit diameter of tortilla. Roll up tortilla jelly-roll fashion. Cut each roll into slices to serve.

Makes 24 to 30 pinwheels

Prep Time: 15 minutes

snappy chicken wings

   24 chicken wings (about 2 pounds)
    ⅔ cup cayenne pepper sauce
    ⅓ cup I CAN'T BELIEVE IT'S NOT BUTTER!® Spread, melted
   1½ teaspoons cayenne pepper
        WISH-BONE® Blue Cheese, Light! Blue Cheese or Fat Free!
        Blue Cheese Dressing

1. Preheat oven to 425°F.

2. Cut tips off wings; cut wings in half at joint. In bowl, combine cayenne pepper sauce, Spread and pepper. Stir in wings until coated.

3. In roasting pan or bottom of broiler pan lined with aluminum foil, arrange wings. Bake 1 hour or until wings are thoroughly cooked and crisp. Serve with Wish-Bone Blue Cheese Dressing. *Makes 48 wings*

Prep Time: 10 minutes
Cook Time: 1 hour

beefy pinwheels

barbecue pizza

2 teaspoons olive oil
1 boneless skinless chicken breast (about 5 ounces), cut into ¾-inch cubes
3 ounces HILLSHIRE FARM® Pepperoni, sliced
⅓ cup barbecue sauce, divided
1 (12-inch) prepared pizza crust
1¼ cups shredded mozzarella cheese, divided
2 tablespoons thinly sliced green onion tops

Preheat oven to 450°F.

Heat oil in small skillet over medium-high heat. Sauté chicken until barely done, 3 to 5 minutes. Remove from heat and pour off juices. Add Pepperoni and 1 tablespoon barbecue sauce to chicken. Stir to mix and separate slices.

Spread remaining barbecue sauce over pizza crust. Sprinkle ¾ cup cheese over sauce. Sprinkle pepperoni mixture over cheese; sprinkle with green onion. Top with remaining ½ cup cheese. Place in oven directly on oven rack. Bake 8 to 10 minutes or until cheese is bubbly and pizza crust is crisp.

Makes 4 to 6 servings

quick tip

*To easily remove a pizza from an oven rack, slide a flat cookie sheet
under the crust and remove the pizza from the oven. Transfer the pizza
to a cutting board and use a pizza cutter to cut into small pieces.*

barbecue pizza

easy sausage empanadas

1 (15-ounce) package refrigerated pie crusts (2 crusts)
¼ pound bulk pork sausage
2 tablespoons finely chopped onion
⅛ teaspoon garlic powder
⅛ teaspoon ground cumin
⅛ teaspoon dried oregano
1 tablespoon chopped pimiento-stuffed green olives
1 tablespoon chopped raisins
1 egg, separated

Let pie crusts stand at room temperature for 20 minutes or according to package directions. Crumble sausage into medium skillet. Add onion, garlic powder, cumin and oregano; cook over medium-high heat until sausage is no longer pink. Drain drippings. Stir in olives and raisins. Lightly beat egg yolk; stir into sausage mixture, mixing well. Carefully unfold crusts. Cut into desired shapes using 3-inch cookie cutters. Place about 2 teaspoons sausage filling on half the cutouts. Top with remaining cutouts. (Or, use round cutter, top with sausage filling and fold dough over to create half-moon shape.) Moisten fingers with water and pinch dough to seal edges. Lightly beat egg white; gently brush over tops of empanadas. Bake in 425°F oven 15 to 18 minutes or until golden brown. *Makes 12 appetizer servings*

Prep Time: 25 minutes
Cook Time: 15 minutes

Favorite recipe from **National Pork Board**

easy sausage empanadas

bacon-wrapped breadsticks

    8 slices bacon
   16 garlic-flavored breadsticks (about 8 inches long)
   ¾ cup grated Parmesan cheese
    2 tablespoons chopped fresh parsley (optional)

1. Cut bacon slices in half lengthwise. Wrap half slice of bacon diagonally around each breadstick. Combine Parmesan cheese and parsley, if desired, in shallow dish; set aside.

2. Place 4 breadsticks on double layer of paper towels in microwave oven. Microwave on HIGH 2 to 3 minutes or until bacon is cooked through. Immediately roll breadsticks in Parmesan mixture to coat. Repeat with remaining breadsticks.   *Makes 16 breadsticks*

spicy mustard kielbasa bites

    1 pound whole kielbasa or smoked Polish sausage
    1 cup *French's*® Spicy Brown Mustard
   ¾ cup honey
    1 tablespoon *Frank's*® *RedHot*® Original Cayenne Pepper Sauce

1. Place kielbasa on grid. Grill over medium heat 10 minutes or until lightly browned, turning occasionally. Cut into bite-sized pieces; set aside.

2. Combine mustard and honey in large saucepan. Bring to a boil over medium heat. Stir in kielbasa and **Frank's RedHot** Sauce. Cook until heated through. Transfer to serving bowl. Serve with party toothpicks.

Makes 8 servings

Tip: Refrigerate leftover honey-mustard mixture. This makes a tasty dip for chicken nuggets, cooked chicken wings or mini hot dogs.

Prep Time: 15 minutes
Cook Time: 10 minutes

bacon-wrapped breadsticks

pork tenderloin sliders

2 tablespoons olive oil, divided
2 pork tenderloins (about 1 pound each)
2 teaspoons chili powder
¾ teaspoon ground cumin
½ teaspoon salt
½ teaspoon black pepper
12 green onions, ends trimmed
½ cup mayonnaise
1 chipotle pepper in adobo sauce, minced
2 teaspoons lime juice
12 dinner rolls, sliced in half horizontally
12 slices Monterey Jack cheese

1. Prepare grill for direct cooking.

2. Rub 1 tablespoon oil evenly over tenderloins. Combine chili powder, cumin, salt and black pepper in small bowl. Sprinkle evenly over tenderloins, pressing to coat all sides of meat. Place onions and remaining 1 tablespoon oil in gallon-size resealable food storage bag. Seal bag; knead to coat onions with oil. Set aside.

3. Place mayonnaise, chipotle pepper and lime juice is small bowl; blend well. Cover and refrigerate.

4. Grill tenderloins on covered grill 15 to 20 minutes or until internal temperature reaches 160°F, turning occasionally. Remove to cutting board. Tent with foil; let stand 10 minutes.

5. Meanwhile, grill onions about 3 minutes or until brown, turning frequently.

6. Coarsely chop grilled onions. Thinly slice tenderloins. Evenly spread chipotle mayonnaise on bottom halves of rolls. Top with onions, tenderloin slices and 1 slice cheese. Replace roll tops. Serve immediately.

Makes 12 sliders

pork tenderloin sliders

tex-mex potato skins

3 hot baked potatoes, split lengthwise
¾ cup (3 ounces) shredded Cheddar or pepper Jack cheese
1⅓ cups *French's®* French Fried Onions, divided
¼ cup chopped green chilies
¼ cup crumbled cooked bacon
   Salsa and sour cream

1. Preheat oven to 350°F. Scoop out inside of potatoes, leaving ¼-inch shells. Reserve inside of potatoes for another use.

2. Arrange potato halves on baking sheet. Top with cheese, ⅔ *cup* French Fried Onions, chilies and bacon.

3. Bake 15 minutes or until heated through and cheese is melted. Cut each potato half crosswise into thirds. Serve topped with salsa, sour cream and remaining onions.   *Makes 18 appetizer servings*

Tip: To bake potatoes quickly, microwave at HIGH 10 to 12 minutes or until tender.

Variation: For added Cheddar flavor, substitute *French's®* **Cheddar French Fried Onions** for the original flavor.

Prep Time: 15 minutes
Cook Time: 15 minutes

tex-mex potato skins

chipotle chicken quesadillas

1 package (8 ounces) cream cheese, softened
1 cup (4 ounces) shredded Mexican Cheddar Jack cheese
1 tablespoon minced chipotle peppers in adobo sauce
5 (10-inch) burrito-size flour tortillas
5 cups shredded cooked chicken (about 1¼ pounds)
   Nonstick cooking spray
   Fresh chopped cilantro (optional)
   Guacamole, sour cream and salsa (optional)

1. Combine cheeses and chipotle peppers in large bowl.

2. Spread ⅓ cup cream cheese mixture over half of tortilla. Top with about 1 cup chicken. Fold over tortilla. Repeat with remaining tortillas.

3. Heat large nonstick skillet over medium-high heat. Spray outside surface of each tortilla with nonstick cooking spray. Cook each tortilla 4 to 6 minutes or until lightly browned, turning once during cooking.

4. Cut each tortilla into 4 wedges. Garnish with cilantro. Serve with guacamole, sour cream and salsa, if desired. *Makes 20 wedges*

quick tip

Chipotle peppers are smoked jalapeño chiles often canned in an adobo sauce which is a dark red Mexican-style sauce made of chili peppers, herbs and vinegar. They can be found in the Mexican food section of your grocery store. If you have leftover chipotle peppers from the can you open for a recipe, they can easily be frozen with the adobo sauce in a food safe container for later use.

chipotle chicken quesadillas

mini marinated beef skewers

    1 boneless beef top sirloin steak (about 1 pound)
    2 tablespoons dry sherry
    2 tablespoons soy sauce
    1 tablespoon dark sesame oil
    2 cloves garlic, minced
   18 cherry tomatoes

1. Cut beef crosswise into ⅛-inch slices. Place in large resealable food storage bag. Combine sherry, soy sauce, sesame oil and garlic in small bowl; pour over beef. Seal bag; turn to coat. Marinate in refrigerator at least 30 minutes or up to 2 hours. Soak 18 (6-inch) wooden skewers in water 20 minutes.

2. Preheat broiler. Drain beef; discard marinade. Weave beef accordion style onto skewers. Place on rack of broiler pan.

3. Broil 4 to 5 inches from heat 4 minutes. Turn skewers over; broil 4 minutes or until beef is barely pink in center. Place 1 cherry tomato on each skewer.

Makes 18 appetizers

refried bean and cheese quesadillas

    1 (16-ounce) can refried beans
    1 tablespoon TABASCO® brand Pepper Sauce
    8 (8-inch) flour tortillas
    1 large red bell pepper, finely chopped
   ¼ cup chopped fresh cilantro or parsley
    2 cups (8 ounces) shredded Monterey Jack or Cheddar cheese

Preheat oven to 450°F. Combine refried beans and TABASCO® Sauce in medium bowl; mix well. Spread 3 tablespoons mixture on each tortilla to within ½ inch of edge; sprinkle with red bell pepper, cilantro and cheese. Place tortillas on 2 large cookie sheets.

Bake 5 minutes or until cheese is melted and edges of tortillas are golden. To serve, cut tortillas into wedges.

Makes 8 quesadillas

mini marinated beef skewers

tuna focaccia melt

1 can (12 ounces) tuna packed in water, drained
⅔ cup *French's® Gourmayo™* Wasabi Horseradish Light Mayonnaise
½ cup finely chopped celery
2 tablespoons minced red or green onion
1 thin pre-baked (12-inch) pizza crust or focaccia bread
2 ripe plum tomatoes, thinly sliced
8 slices Swiss, American, Muenster, or mozzarella cheese

1. Heat oven to 450°F. Mix tuna, mayonnaise, celery and onion in large bowl until well blended. Spread on pizza shell. Arrange tomato slices and cheese on top.

2. Place pizza crust on pizza pan. Bake 10 minutes or until cheese is melted. Cut into wedges to serve. Garnish as desired.   *Makes 8 servings*

Variations: Substitute any flavor of **French's® Gourmayo™** Light Mayonnaise. For a change of pace, substitute 2 cups shredded chicken for the tuna.

Prep Time: 10 minutes
Cook Time: 10 minutes

pizza-stuffed mushrooms

12 large or 24 medium fresh mushrooms
¼ cup chopped green bell pepper
¼ cup chopped pepperoni or cooked, crumbled Italian sausage
1 cup (½ of 15-ounce can) CONTADINA® Pizza Sauce
½ cup (2 ounces) shredded mozzarella cheese

1. Wash and dry mushrooms; remove stems. Chop ¼ cup stems. In small bowl, combine chopped stems, bell pepper, meat and pizza sauce. Spoon mixture into mushroom caps; top with cheese.

2. Broil 6 to 8 inches from heat for 2 to 3 minutes or until cheese is melted and mushrooms are heated through.   *Makes 12 or 24 mushrooms*

Prep Time: 15 minutes
Cook Time: 3 minutes

mini sausage quiches

½ **cup butter or margarine, softened**
3 **ounces cream cheese, softened**
1 **cup all-purpose flour**
½ **pound BOB EVANS® Italian Roll Sausage**
1 **cup (4 ounces) shredded Swiss cheese**
1 **tablespoon snipped fresh chives**
2 **eggs**
1 **cup half-and-half**
¼ **teaspoon salt**
   Dash cayenne pepper

Beat butter and cream cheese in medium bowl until creamy. Blend in flour; refrigerate 1 hour. Roll into 24 (1-inch) balls; press each into ungreased mini-muffin cup to form pastry shell. Preheat oven to 375°F. To prepare filling, crumble sausage into small skillet. Cook over medium heat until browned, stirring occasionally. Drain off any drippings. Sprinkle evenly into pastry shells in muffin cups; sprinkle with Swiss cheese and chives. Whisk eggs, half-and-half, salt and cayenne until blended; pour into pastry shells. Bake 20 to 30 minutes or until set. Remove from pans. Serve hot. Refrigerate leftovers.   *Makes 24 appetizers*

quick tip

*To make larger quiches for breakfast, roll dough into 12 (2-inch) balls;
press each into ungreased standard muffins cup to form pastry shell.
Divide sausage and egg mixture evenly among muffin cups. Bake in
preheated 375°F oven 25 minutes or until set.*

easy spinach appetizer

2 tablespoons butter

3 eggs

1 cup all-purpose flour

1 cup milk

1 teaspoon baking powder

1 teaspoon salt

2 packages (10 ounces each) frozen chopped spinach, thawed
    and well drained

4 cups (16 ounces) shredded Monterey Jack cheese

½ cup diced red bell pepper

1. Preheat oven to 350°F. Melt butter in 13×9-inch baking pan.

2. Beat eggs in medium bowl. Add flour, milk, baking powder and salt; beat until well blended. Stir in spinach, cheese and bell pepper; mix well. Spread mixture in pan.

3. Bake 40 to 45 minutes or until set. Let stand 10 minutes; cut into triangles or squares to serve. *Makes 2 to 4 dozen pieces*

quick tip

This delicious appetizer can also be made ahead, frozen and reheated. After baking, cool completely and cut into squares. Transfer the squares to a baking sheet; place it in the freezer until the squares are frozen solid. Transfer to a large resealable food storage bag. To serve, reheat the squares in a preheated 325°F oven for 15 minutes.

easy spinach appetizer

original buffalo chicken wings

Zesty Blue Cheese Dip (recipe follows)
2½ pounds chicken wings, split and tips discarded
½ cup *Frank's® RedHot®* Original Cayenne Pepper Sauce (or to taste)
⅓ cup butter or margarine, melted
Celery sticks

1. Prepare Zesty Blue Cheese Dip.

2. Deep fry wings at 400°F 12 minutes or until crisp and no longer pink; drain.

3. Combine **Frank's RedHot** Sauce and butter in large bowl. Add wings to sauce; toss well to coat evenly. Serve with Zesty Blue Cheese Dip and celery.

Makes 24 to 30 individual pieces

To Broil: Place wings in single layer on rack in foil-lined roasting pan. Broil 6 inches from heat 15 to 20 minutes or until crisp and no longer pink, turning once halfway through cooking time.

zesty blue cheese dip

½ cup blue cheese salad dressing
¼ cup sour cream
2 teaspoons *Frank's® RedHot®* Original Cayenne Pepper Sauce

Combine all ingredients in medium serving bow; mix well. Garnish with crumbled blue cheese, if desired.

Makes ¾ cup dip

Cajun Wings: Cook chicken wings as directed above. Combine ⅓ cup **Frank's RedHot** Sauce, ⅓ cup ketchup, ¼ cup (½ stick) melted butter or margarine and 2 teaspoons Cajun seasoning in small bowl. Mix well. Pour sauce over wings; toss well to coat evenly.

Santa Fe Wings: Cook chicken wings as directed above. Combine ¼ cup (½ stick) melted butter or margarine, ¼ cup **Frank's RedHot** Sauce, ¼ cup ketchup, ⅓ cup chili sauce and 1 teaspoon chili powder in small bowl. Mix well. Pour sauce over wings; toss well to coat evenly.

original buffalo chicken wings

french-style pizza bites

2 tablespoons olive oil
1 medium onion, thinly sliced
1 medium red bell pepper, cut into 3-inch-long strips
2 cloves garlic, minced
⅓ cup pitted black olives, cut into thin wedges
1 package (13.8 ounces) refrigerated pizza crust dough
¾ cup (3 ounces) finely shredded Swiss or Gruyère cheese

1. Position oven rack to lowest position. Preheat oven to 425°F.

2. Heat oil in medium skillet over medium heat. Add onion, bell pepper and garlic. Cook and stir 5 minutes or until crisp-tender. Stir in olives. Remove from heat; set aside.

3. Pat dough into 16×12-inch rectangle on greased large baking sheet. Arrange onion mixture over dough. Sprinkle with cheese. Bake 10 minutes. Loosen crust from baking sheet. Slide crust onto oven rack. Bake 3 to 5 minutes more or until golden brown.

4. Slide baking sheet under crust; remove crust from rack. Transfer to cutting board. Cut dough crosswise into eight 1¾-inch-wide strips. Cut dough diagonally into ten 2-inch-wide strips, making diamond pieces. Serve immediately. *Makes about 24 pieces*

ham and cherry roll-ups

1 package (8 ounces) cream cheese, softened
½ cup sliced green onions
½ cup toasted chopped walnuts
¼ cup cherry preserves
1 pound sliced deli ham (16 to 20 slices)

In small bowl, stir together all ingredients except ham. Spread a rounded tablespoon of the cream cheese mixture on each ham slice. Roll up; cut each roll in half. Secure rolls with wooden picks. Refrigerate, covered, until serving time. *Makes 32 to 40 appetizers*

Tip: Prepare and refrigerate these easy appetizers up to 1 day ahead.

Favorite recipe from **National Pork Board**

french-style pizza bites

micro mini stuffed potatoes

1 pound small new potatoes, scrubbed
¼ cup sour cream
2 tablespoons butter, softened
½ teaspoon minced garlic
¼ cup milk
½ cup (2 ounces) shredded sharp Cheddar cheese
½ teaspoon salt
¼ teaspoon black pepper
¼ cup finely chopped green onion (optional)

1. Pierce potatoes with fork in several places. Microwave potatoes on HIGH 5 to 6 minutes or until tender. Let stand 5 minutes; cut in half lengthwise. Scoop out pulp from potatoes and place in medium bowl.

2. Beat potatoes with electric mixer at low speed 30 seconds. Add sour cream, butter and garlic; beat until well blended. Gradually add milk, beating until smooth. Add cheese, salt and pepper; beat until blended.

3. Fill each potato shell with equal amounts of potato mixture. Microwave on HIGH 1 to 2 minutes or just until cheese melts. Garnish with green onions.

Makes 4 to 8 servings

micro mini stuffed potatoes

individual spinach & bacon quiches

3 slices bacon
½ small onion, diced
1 package (10 ounces) frozen chopped spinach, thawed and squeezed dry
½ teaspoon black pepper
⅛ teaspoon ground nutmeg
    Pinch salt
1 container (15 ounces) whole milk ricotta cheese
2 cups (8 ounces) shredded mozzarella cheese
1 cup grated Parmesan cheese
3 eggs, lightly beaten

1. Preheat oven to 350°F. Spray 10 standard (2½-inch) muffin cups with nonstick cooking spray.

2. Cook bacon in large skillet over medium-high heat until crisp. Drain on paper towels. Let bacon cool; crumble.

3. In same skillet, cook and stir onion 5 minutes or until tender. Add spinach, pepper, nutmeg and salt. Cook and stir over medium heat about 3 minutes or until liquid evaporates. Remove from heat. Stir in bacon; cool.

4. Combine cheeses in large bowl. Add eggs; stir until well blended. Add cooled spinach mixture; mix well.

5. Divide mixture evenly among prepared muffin cups. Bake 40 minutes or until filling is set. Let stand 10 minutes. Run knife around edges to release. Serve hot or refrigerate and serve cold.   *Makes 10 servings*

individual spinach & bacon quiches

fancy party
noshes

pineapple-scallop bites

½ cup *French's®* Honey Dijon Mustard
¼ cup orange marmalade
1 cup canned pineapple cubes (24 pieces)
12 sea scallops (8 ounces), cut in half crosswise
12 strips (6 ounces) uncooked turkey bacon, cut in half crosswise*

*Or, substitute regular bacon for turkey bacon. Simmer 5 minutes in enough boiling water to cover; drain well before wrapping scallops.

1. Soak 12 (6-inch) bamboo skewers in hot water 20 minutes. Combine mustard and marmalade in small bowl. Reserve ½ cup mustard mixture for dipping sauce.

2. Hold 1 pineapple cube and 1 scallop half together. Wrap with 1 bacon strip. Thread onto skewer. Repeat with remaining pineapple, scallops and bacon.

3. Place skewers on oiled grid. Grill over medium heat 6 minutes, turning frequently and brushing with remaining mustard mixture. Serve hot with reserved dipping sauce. *Makes 6 to 12 servings*

Prep Time: 25 minutes
Cook Time: 6 minutes

pineapple-scallop bites

beer and coconut-macadamia shrimp

1 pound large raw shrimp, peeled and deveined (with tails on)
1½ teaspoons salt, divided
   Ground red pepper
½ cup all-purpose flour
¼ teaspoon white pepper
1 cup sweetened shredded coconut
⅔ cup panko (Japanese-style) bread crumbs
½ cup finely chopped macadamia nuts
2 eggs, beaten
¼ cup wheat beer
1 cup peanut oil
   Apricot or pineapple preserves

1. Spread shrimp on paper towels and pat dry. Season with ½ teaspoon salt and red pepper.

2. Combine flour, remaining 1 teaspoon salt and white pepper in shallow dish; set aside. Combine coconut, bread crumbs and macadamia nuts in shallow dish; set aside. Beat eggs and beer in small bowl; set aside.

3. Heat oil in heavy saucepan over medium-high heat to 350°F.

4. Working in small batches, dredge shrimp in flour mixture. Dip in egg mixture and roll in coconut mixture. Place carefully in oil, frying 2 minutes per side. Drain in paper towel-lined colander. Use a slotted spoon to remove extra pieces of coconut from oil. Fry remaining shrimp.

5. Serve immediately with preserves. *Makes 6 to 8 servings*

beer and coconut-macadamia shrimp

marinated antipasto

¼ cup extra-virgin olive oil

2 tablespoons balsamic vinegar

1 clove garlic, minced

½ teaspoon sugar

½ teaspoon salt

¼ teaspoon black pepper

1 pint (2 cups) cherry tomatoes

1 can (14 ounces) quartered artichoke hearts, drained

8 ounces small balls or cubes fresh mozzarella cheese

1 cup drained whole pitted kalamata olives

¼ cup chopped fresh basil

Lettuce leaves

1. Whisk together oil, vinegar, garlic, sugar, salt and pepper in medium bowl. Add tomatoes, artichokes, mozzarella, olives and basil; toss to coat. Let stand at least 30 minutes.

2. Serve on lettuce-lined platter at room temperature.

Makes about 5 cups (12 appetizer servings)

cheesy christmas trees

½ cup mayonnaise

1 tablespoon dry ranch-style salad dressing mix

1 cup (4 ounces) shredded Cheddar cheese

¼ cup grated Parmesan cheese

12 slices firm white bread

¼ cup red bell pepper strips

¼ cup green bell pepper strips

1. Preheat broiler. Combine mayonnaise and dressing mix in medium bowl. Add cheeses; mix well.

2. Cut bread slices into Christmas tree shapes using cookie cutters. Spread about 1 tablespoon mayonnaise mixture over each tree. Decorate with red and green bell pepper strips. Place on baking sheet. Broil 4 inches from heat 2 to 3 minutes or until bubbling. Serve warm.

Makes about 12 appetizers

marinated antipasto

crab and artichoke stuffed mushrooms

½ **pound Florida blue crab meat**
1 **(14-ounce) can artichoke hearts, drained and finely chopped**
1 **cup mayonnaise***
½ **cup grated Parmesan cheese**
¼ **teaspoon lemon pepper seasoning**
⅛ **teaspoon salt**
⅛ **teaspoon cayenne pepper**
30 **large fresh Florida mushrooms**

Or, you can substitute mixture of ½ cup mayonnaise and ½ cup plain yogurt.

Remove any pieces of shell or cartilage from crabmeat. Combine crabmeat, artichoke hearts, mayonnaise, Parmesan cheese and seasonings; mix until well blended. Remove stems from mushrooms and fill the caps with crabmeat mixture. Place in a lightly greased, shallow baking dish. Bake in a preheated 400°F oven for 10 minutes or until hot and bubbly.   *Makes 30 appetizers*

Favorite recipe from **Florida Department of Agriculture and Consumer Services, Bureau of Seafood and Aquaculture**

smoked salmon roses

1 **package (8 ounces) cream cheese, softened**
1 **tablespoon prepared horseradish**
1 **tablespoon minced fresh dill**
1 **tablespoon half-and-half**
16 **slices (12 to 16 ounces) smoked salmon**
1 **red bell pepper, cut into thin strips**
  Fresh dill sprigs

1. Combine cream cheese, horseradish, minced dill and half-and-half in small bowl. Beat until light and creamy.

2. Spread 1 tablespoon cream cheese mixture over each salmon slice. Roll up jelly-roll style. Slice each roll in half crosswise. Arrange salmon rolls, cut sides down, on serving dish to resemble roses. Place pepper strips and dill sprig in center of each rose.   *Makes 32 servings*

crab and artichoke stuffed mushrooms

marinated artichoke cheese toasts

1 jar (about 6 ounces) marinated artichoke hearts, drained
½ cup (2 ounces) shredded Swiss cheese
⅓ cup finely chopped roasted red peppers
⅓ cup finely chopped celery
1 tablespoon plus 1½ teaspoons mayonnaise
24 melba toast rounds
Paprika (optional)

1. Rinse artichokes under cold running water; drain well. Pat dry with paper towels. Finely chop artichokes; place in medium bowl. Add cheese, peppers, celery and mayonnaise; mix well.

2. Spoon artichoke mixture evenly onto melba toast rounds; place on large nonstick baking sheet or broiler pan. Broil 6 inches from heat 45 seconds or until cheese mixture is hot and bubbly. Garnish with paprika.

Makes 24 toasts

alouette® crème de brie® appetizers with caramelized onion

1 tablespoon butter
1 large sweet onion (preferably Vidalia), diced
2 teaspoons sugar
1 (2.1-ounce) box frozen prebaked phyllo tartlet shells
1 (5-ounce) package ALOUETTE® Crème de Brie®, any variety
2 tablespoons chopped fresh parsley

Preheat oven to 375°F. Melt butter in small skillet over medium heat. Add onion and sauté until golden. Just when onion begins to brown, sprinkle with sugar and continue cooking until golden brown. Fill each phyllo shell with heaping teaspoon *Crème de Brie®* and top with ½ teaspoon caramelized onion. Place on baking sheet; warm in oven about 5 minutes. Garnish with parsley and serve immediately.

Makes 15 appetizers

marinated artichoke cheese toasts

santa fe shrimp martini cocktails

1 jar (16 ounces) mild salsa

1 small ripe avocado, peeled and chopped

1 tablespoon chopped fresh cilantro leaves

1 tablespoon *Frank's® RedHot®* Original Cayenne Pepper Sauce

1 tablespoon lime juice

1 pound large shrimp, cooked, peeled and deveined

1 cup *French's®* French Fried Onions

1 lime, cut into 6 wedges

1. Combine salsa, avocado, cilantro, **Frank's RedHot** Sauce and lime juice in large bowl. Alternately layer shrimp and salsa mixture in 6 martini or margarita glasses.

2. Microwave French Fried Onions on HIGH for 1 minute until golden. Sprinkle over shrimp. Garnish with lime wedges.   *Makes 6 servings*

Prep Time: 10 minutes
Cook Time: 1 minute

quick tip

For a quick to fix shrimp cocktail, purchase cooked cleaned shrimp from the seafood section of your local supermarket. Or, purchase frozen cooked shrimp and thaw according to package directions.

santa fe shrimp martini cocktails and crab cakes
with horseradish mustard sauce *(page 97)*

wisconsin swiss fondue

2 cups dry white wine
1 tablespoon lemon juice
1 pound Wisconsin Gruyère cheese, shredded
1 pound Wisconsin Fontina cheese, shredded
1 tablespoon arrowroot
2 ounces kirsch
    Pinch of ground nutmeg
    French bread cubes
    Pears, cut into wedges
    Apples, cut into wedges

Bring wine and lemon juice to a boil in fondue pot. Reduce heat to low. Toss cheeses with arrowroot. Gradually add to wine mixture, stirring constantly. When cheese is completely melted, stir in kirsch. Sprinkle with nutmeg and serve with French bread cubes, pears and apples.   *Makes 6 servings*

Favorite recipe from **Wisconsin Milk Marketing Board**

oysters romano

12 oysters, shucked and on the half shell
 2 slices bacon, cut into 12 (1-inch) pieces
½ cup Italian-seasoned dry bread crumbs
 2 tablespoons butter or margarine, melted
½ teaspoon garlic salt
 6 tablespoons grated Romano or Parmesan cheese
    Minced fresh chives (optional)

1. Preheat oven to 375°F. Place shells with oysters on baking sheet. Top each oyster with 1 piece bacon. Bake 10 minutes or until bacon is crisp.

2. Meanwhile, combine bread crumbs, butter and garlic salt in small bowl. Spoon mixture over oysters; sprinkle with cheese. Bake 5 to 10 minutes or until cheese melts. Garnish with chives.   *Makes 12 appetizers*

crab cakes
with horseradish mustard sauce

Horseradish Mustard Sauce

- ½ **cup mayonnaise**
- 2 **tablespoons** *French's*® **Honey Dijon Mustard**
- 1 **tablespoon prepared horseradish**

Crab Cakes

- 1⅓ **cups** *French's*® **French Fried Onions, divided**
- 3 **cans (6 ounces each) jumbo lump crabmeat, drained**
- ¼ **cup unseasoned dry bread crumbs**
- ¼ **cup mayonnaise**
- 1 **egg, slightly beaten**
- 2 **tablespoons chopped pimentos**
- 2 **tablespoons chopped fresh parsley**
- 1 **tablespoon** *French's*® **Honey Dijon Mustard**
- 1 **tablespoon prepared horseradish**
- 1 **teaspoon minced garlic**

1. Combine ingredients for Horseradish Mustard Sauce in small bowl. Chill until ready to serve.

2. Lightly crush ⅔ cup French Fried Onions. Place in large bowl. Add remaining ingredients for crab cakes; mix until well combined. Shape mixture into cakes using about ¼ cup mixture for each; flatten slightly.

3. Heat 2 tablespoons oil in 12-inch nonstick skillet over medium high heat. Cook crab cakes in batches about 2 to 3 minutes per side or until golden. Drain. Transfer crab cakes to serving platter. Serve each crab cake topped with Horseradish Mustard Sauce and remaining onions.

Makes about 12 crab cakes

spinach-artichoke party cups

Nonstick cooking spray
36 (3-inch) wonton wrappers
1 jar (about 6 ounces) marinated artichoke hearts, drained and chopped
½ (10-ounce) package frozen chopped spinach, thawed and squeezed dry
1 cup (4 ounces) shredded Monterey Jack cheese
½ cup grated Parmesan cheese
½ cup mayonnaise
1 clove garlic, minced

1. Preheat oven to 300°F. Spray mini (1¾-inch) muffin cups lightly with cooking spray. Press 1 wonton wrapper into each cup; spray lightly with cooking spray. Bake about 9 minutes or until light golden brown. Remove shells from pan; place on wire rack to cool. Repeat with remaining wonton wrappers.*

2. Meanwhile, combine artichoke hearts, spinach, cheeses, mayonnaise and garlic in medium bowl; mix well.

3. Fill each wonton cup with about 1½ teaspoons spinach-artichoke mixture. Place filled cups on baking sheet. Bake about 7 minutes or until heated through. Serve immediately. *Makes 36 appetizers*

Wonton cups may be prepared up to one week in advance. Cool completely and store in an airtight container.

quick tip

If you have leftover spinach-artichoke mixture after filling the wonton cups, place the mixture in a shallow ovenproof dish and bake in a preheated 350°F oven until hot and bubbly. Serve it with bread or crackers.

spinach-artichoke party cups

baked brie

½ **pound Brie cheese, rind removed**
¼ **cup chopped pecans**
¼ **cup KARO® Dark Corn Syrup**

1. Preheat oven to 350°F. Place cheese in shallow oven-safe serving dish. Top with pecans and corn syrup.

2. Bake 8 to 10 minutes or until cheese is almost melted. Serve warm with plain crackers or melba toast. *Makes 8 servings*

Prep Time: 3 minutes
Cook Time: 10 minutes

salmon appetizers

1 **package frozen puff pastry sheets, thawed**
4 **ounces smoked salmon, flaked**
8 **ounces cream cheese, softened**
2 **tablespoons snipped fresh chives**
1½ **teaspoons lemon juice**

Preheat oven to 375°F. Cut twelve 2-inch rounds of dough from pastry sheet; place in greased muffin cups. (Freeze remaining pastry sheet for later use.) Top dough rounds with salmon. Mix cream cheese, chives and lemon juice until creamy. Top salmon with about 1 tablespoon cream cheese mixture or pipe cream cheese over salmon, if desired. Bake 15 to 18 minutes. Serve warm. *Makes 12 appetizers*

Favorite recipe from **Wisconsin Milk Marketing Board**

baked brie

asparagus & prosciutto antipasto

12 fresh asparagus spears (about 8 ounces)
2 ounces cream cheese, softened
¼ cup crumbled blue cheese or goat cheese
¼ teaspoon black pepper
1 package (3 to 4 ounces) thinly sliced prosciutto

1. Trim off and discard tough bottoms of asparagus spears. Simmer asparagus in salted water in large skillet 4 to 5 minutes or until crisp-tender. Drain; immediately immerse in cold water to stop cooking.

2. Meanwhile, combine cheeses and pepper in small bowl; mix well. Cut prosciutto slices in half crosswise to make 12 pieces. Spread cream cheese mixture evenly over one side of each prosciutto piece.

3. Drain asparagus; pat dry with paper towels. Wrap each asparagus spear with one piece prosciutto. Serve at room temperature or slightly chilled.

Makes 12 appetizers

basil'd cream cheese with capers

6 ounces baguette bread, cut into 32 slices
1 container (8 ounces) garlic and herb cream cheese
3 tablespoons chopped fresh basil
2 tablespoons capers, drained
1 clove garlic, halved crosswise

1. Preheat oven to 350°F.

2. Arrange bread slices on baking sheet; bake 5 minutes. Turn and bake 5 minutes more or until beginning to turn golden around edges. Cool completely.

3. Combine cheese, basil and capers in small bowl. Stir until well blended.

4. Rub cut side of garlic on one side of each bread slice; discard garlic.

5. Serve cheese mixture with bread slices.

Makes 1 cup dip

Variation: Serve cheese mixture on water crackers or cherry tomato halves.

asparagus & prosciutto antipasto

tuna in crispy wonton cups

18 wonton skins, each 3¼ inches square
   Butter or olive oil cooking spray
 1 (3-ounce) STARKIST Flavor Fresh Pouch® Tuna (Albacore or Chunk Light)
 ⅓ cup cold cooked orzo (rice-shaped pasta) or cooked rice
 ¼ cup southwestern ranch-style vegetable dip with jalapeños or other sour cream dip
 ¼ cup drained pimiento-stuffed green olives, chopped
 3 tablespoons sweet pickle relish, drained
   Paprika, for garnish
   Parsley sprigs, for garnish

Cut wontons into circles with 3-inch round cookie cutter. Spray miniature muffin pans with cooking spray. Place one circle in each muffin cup; press to sides to mold wonton to cup. Spray each wonton with cooking spray. Bake in 350°F oven 6 to 8 minutes or until golden brown; set aside.

In small bowl, gently mix tuna, orzo, dip, olives and relish. Refrigerate filling until ready to serve. Remove wonton cups from muffin pan. Use rounded teaspoon to fill each cup; garnish with paprika and parsley.

Makes 18 servings

Prep Time: 20 minutes

quick tip

*Wonton cups can be made up to one week in advance.
Cool completely and store in an airtight container.
Reheat in 350°F oven 1 to 2 minutes until crisp.*

tuna in crispy wonton cups

hot pepper cranberry jelly appetizer

½ **cup whole berry cranberry sauce**
¼ **cup apricot fruit spread**
1 **teaspoon sugar**
1 **teaspoon cider vinegar**
½ **teaspoon red pepper flakes**
½ **teaspoon grated fresh ginger**
   Assorted crackers
   Assorted sliced cheeses

1. Combine cranberry sauce, fruit spread, sugar, vinegar and pepper flakes in small saucepan. Cook over medium heat until sugar has dissolved; do not boil. Transfer to bowl; cool completely. Stir in ginger.

2. To serve, top crackers with cheese slices and spoonful of cranberry-apricot mixture.   *Makes 16 appetizer servings*

spicy marinated shrimp

1 **green onion, finely chopped**
2 **tablespoons olive oil**
2 **tablespoons fresh lemon juice**
2 **tablespoons prepared horseradish**
2 **tablespoons ketchup**
1 **tablespoon finely chopped fresh chives**
1 **teaspoon TABASCO® brand Pepper Sauce**
1 **teaspoon Dijon mustard**
1 **clove garlic, minced**
   Salt to taste
2 **pounds medium shrimp, cooked, peeled and deveined**

Combine all ingredients except shrimp in large bowl. Add shrimp and toss to coat. Cover and refrigerate 4 to 6 hours or overnight. Transfer shrimp mixture to serving bowl and serve with toothpicks.   *Makes 30 to 40 shrimp*

hot pepper cranberry jelly appetizer

crunchy
munchies

super bowl snack mix

1½ cups raw almonds
1 cup shelled raw pistachios
1 cup dried cherries
½ cup packed brown sugar
1 teaspoon chili powder
½ teaspoon salt
½ teaspoon curry powder
½ teaspoon five-spice powder
1 egg white

1. Preheat oven to 250°F.

2. Combine almonds, pistachios, cherries, brown sugar, chili powder, salt, curry powder and five-spice powder in medium bowl; stir well.

3. Whisk egg white in large bowl until frothy. Add nut mixture; stir gently to coat.

4. Spread mixture evenly onto nonstick baking sheet. Bake 35 to 40 minutes, stirring occasionally. Let mixture cool 30 minutes or until syrup is firm. Break into small chunks. Store mix in airtight container.   *Makes about 4 cups*

super bowl snack mix

crunchy-fruity snack mix

1 cup (4 ounces) roasted and salted soy nuts
1 cup broken-in-half pretzel sticks (about 1½ ounces)
⅔ cup white chocolate chips
⅔ cup dried pineapple, cut into ½-inch pieces
⅔ cup dried cranberries

Combine all ingredients in large bowl; mix well. Store in airtight container up to 7 days. *Makes about 4 cups*

glitterrazzi popcorn

1 bag popped JOLLY TIME® Blast O Butter Microwave Popcorn (about 10-12 cups)
1 cup salted mixed nuts
½ cup dried cranberries
1 package (12 ounces) white (vanilla flavored) baking chips
½ teaspoon ground cinnamon
Edible gold powder (optional)

1. Pop popcorn according to package directions. Open bag carefully and pour into large bowl; discard unpopped kernels.

2. Add nuts and cranberries to bowl with popcorn; stir well.

3. In microwave oven or double boiler, melt chips according to package directions.

4. Pour over popcorn mixture; stir until evenly coated.

5. Spread onto large rimmed baking sheet; sprinkle with cinnamon, stirring to distribute evenly. Cool completely. Sprinkle with gold powder, if desired. Store tightly covered.

6. Serve in martini glass for unique presentation. *Makes 6 servings*

crunchy-fruity snack mix

teddy bear party mix

4 cups crisp cinnamon graham cereal
2 cups honey flavored teddy-shaped graham snacks
1 can (1½ ounces) *French's®* Potato Sticks
3 tablespoons melted unsalted butter
2 tablespoons *French's®* Worcestershire Sauce
1 tablespoon packed brown sugar
¼ teaspoon ground cinnamon
1 cup sweetened dried cranberries or raisins
½ cup chocolate, peanut butter or carob chips

1. Preheat oven to 350°F. Lightly spray jelly-roll pan with nonstick cooking spray. Combine cereal, graham snacks and potato sticks in large bowl.

2. Combine butter, Worcestershire, sugar and cinnamon in small bowl; toss with cereal mixture. Transfer to prepared pan. Bake 12 minutes. Cool completely.

3. Stir in dried cranberries and chips. Store in an airtight container.

Makes about 7 cups

Prep Time: 5 minutes
Cook Time: 12 minutes

cheesy chips

10 wonton wrappers
2 tablespoons grated Parmesan cheese
2 teaspoons olive oil
⅛ teaspoon garlic powder

1. Preheat oven to 375°F. Spray baking sheet with nonstick cooking spray.

2. Diagonally cut each wonton wrapper in half, forming two triangles. Place in single layer on prepared baking sheet.

3. Combine cheese, oil and garlic powder in small bowl. Sprinkle over wonton triangles. Bake 6 to 8 minutes or until golden brown and crisp. Remove from oven. Cool completely.

Makes 20 chips

teddy bear party mix

taco popcorn olé

  9 cups air-popped popcorn
    Butter-flavored cooking spray
  1 teaspoon chili powder
  ½ teaspoon salt
  ½ teaspoon garlic powder
  ⅛ teaspoon ground red pepper (optional)

1. Preheat oven to 350°F. Line 15×10-inch jelly-roll pan with foil.

2. Place popcorn in single layer on prepared pan. Coat lightly with cooking spray.

3. Combine chili powder, salt, garlic powder and red pepper, if desired, in small bowl; sprinkle over popcorn. Mix lightly to coat evenly.

4. Bake 5 minutes or until hot, stirring gently after 3 minutes. Cool.

Makes 6 servings

peanut butter
peanut caramel popcorn

  ½ cup KARO® Light or Dark Corn Syrup
  ½ cup sugar
  ⅔ cup creamy or chunky peanut butter
  ½ teaspoon salt
  8 cups popped popcorn

Microwave Directions

In a 3-quart microwave bowl, combine corn syrup and sugar. Microwave on High (100%) 2 minutes or until mixture boils. Stir in peanut butter and ½ teaspoon salt.

Immediately stir in popped popcorn; toss to coat. Microwave stirring twice at 5 minute intervals. Store in airtight container. *Makes 2 quarts*

Prep Time: 10 minutes

taco popcorn olé

nutty onion snack mix

1 can (6 ounces) *French's®* French Fried Onions
2 cups mixed nuts
1½ cups small pretzel twists
2 cans (1½ ounces each) *French's®* Potato Sticks
3 tablespoons butter or margarine, melted
3 tablespoons *French's®* Spicy Brown Mustard

1. Place French Fried Onions, nuts, pretzels and potato sticks in 4-quart microwave-safe bowl. Combine butter and mustard. Pour over mixture in bowl; toss well to coat evenly.

2. Microwave, uncovered, on HIGH for 6 minutes, stirring well every 2 minutes. Transfer to paper towels; cool completely.

Makes about 9 cups

Prep Time: 5 minutes
Cook Time: 6 minutes

zesty buffalo style popcorn

3 tablespoons hot-pepper jelly
1 teaspoon Cajun seasoning
1 tablespoon zero-calorie margarine cooking spray
1 bag (3 ounces) JOLLY TIME® Healthy Pop 94% Fat Free Microwave Popcorn, popped
20 baked ranch-flavored crackers
16 reduced-fat cheese snack crackers

1. In a small bowl, combine jelly, Cajun seasoning and margarine spray; mix well.

2. Place popped popcorn in a large bowl, removing any unpoppped kernels. Add ranch and cheese crackers, toss to combine. Drizzle with jelly mixture. Transfer to two 9-inch microwave-safe pie pans. Microwave each on high for 1½ minutes, stirring halfway through cooking time.

3. Transfer to waxed paper to cool. *Makes 9 (1 cup) servings*

Prep Time: 10 minutes

chocolate & fruit snack mix

½ cup (1 stick) butter or margarine
2 tablespoons sugar
1 tablespoon HERSHEY'S Cocoa or HERSHEY'S SPECIAL DARK® Cocoa
½ teaspoon ground cinnamon
3 cups bite-size crisp rice squares cereal
3 cups bite-size crisp wheat squares cereal
2 cups toasted oat cereal rings
1 cup cashews
1½ cups (6-ounce package) dried fruit bits
1 cup HERSHEY'S Semi-Sweet Chocolate Chips

1. Place butter in 4-quart microwave-safe bowl. Microwave at HIGH (100%) 1 minute or until melted; stir in sugar, cocoa and cinnamon. Add cereals and cashews; stir until evenly coated. Microwave at HIGH 3 minutes, stirring after each minute; stir in dried fruit. Microwave at HIGH 3 minutes, stirring after each minute.

2. Cool completely; stir in chocolate chips. Store in tightly covered container in cool, dry place. *Makes about 11 cups*

sweet nothings trail mix

5 cups rice and corn cereal squares
1½ cups raisins
1½ cups small thin pretzel sticks, broken into pieces
1 cup candy-coated chocolate pieces
1 cup peanuts

1. Decorate small resealable food storage bags with Valentine's Day stickers, if desired.

2. Combine cereal, raisins, pretzels, chocolate pieces and peanuts in large resealable food storage bag; shake well. Distribute evenly among decorated bags or serve in large bowl. *Makes 10 (1-cup) servings*

Serve It With Style!: If you'd rather use this recipe as a party favor, wrap handfuls of trail mix in pink plastic wrap and tie with red, white or pink ribbons.

Prep and Cook Time: 10 minutes

honey crunch popcorn

3 quarts (12 cups) hot air-popped popcorn
½ cup chopped pecans
½ cup packed brown sugar
½ cup honey

1. Preheat oven to 300°F. Spray large nonstick baking sheet with nonstick cooking spray.

2. Combine popcorn and pecans in large bowl; mix lightly. Set aside.

3. Combine brown sugar and honey in small saucepan. Cook over medium heat just until brown sugar is dissolved and mixture comes to a boil, stirring occasionally. Pour over popcorn mixture; toss lightly to coat evenly. Transfer to prepared baking sheet.

4. Bake 30 minutes, stirring after 15 minutes. Spray large sheet of waxed paper with nonstick cooking spray. Transfer popcorn to prepared waxed paper to cool. Store in airtight containers.   *Makes about 12 cups*

Variation: Add 1 cup chopped mixed dried fruit immediately after removing popcorn from oven.

everything but the kitchen sink

1 cup candy-coated chocolate candies
1 cup SUN•MAID® Raisins
1 cup dry roasted peanuts
1 cup round toasted oat cereal
1 cup miniature pretzel twists

In large self-sealing plastic bag, **PLACE** candy coated chocolate candies, raisins and peanuts. **SEAL** bag and gently **ROTATE** to mix together.

Just before serving, **STIR** in toasted oat cereal and mini pretzel twists.

Makes 5 cups

honey crunch popcorn

sweet & spicy beer nuts

2 cups pecan halves
2 teaspoons salt
2 teaspoons chili powder
2 teaspoons olive oil
½ teaspoon ground cumin
¼ teaspoon ground red pepper
½ cup sugar
½ cup beer

1. Preheat oven to 350°F. Line baking sheet with foil.

2. Combine pecans, salt, chili powder, oil, cumin and red pepper in small bowl. Spread onto prepared baking sheet. Toast 10 minutes or until fragrant. Cool in pan on wire rack.

3. Combine sugar and beer in small saucepan. Heat over medium-high heat until mixture registers 250°F on candy thermometer. Remove from heat; carefully stir in nuts and any loose spices. Spread sugared nuts on foil-lined baking sheet, separating clusters.

4. Let cool. Break up large pieces before serving.   *Makes 3 cups*

peanut butter 'n' chocolate chips snack mix

6 cups bite-size crisp corn, rice or wheat squares cereal
3 cups miniature pretzels
2 cups toasted oat cereal rings
1 cup raisins or dried fruit bits
1 cup HERSHEY₅'S Semi-Sweet Chocolate Chips
1 cup REESE'S® Peanut Butter Chips

Stir together all ingredients in large bowl. Store in airtight container at room temperature.   *Makes 14 cups*

sweet & spicy beer nuts

popcorn granola

6 cups air-popped popcorn
1 cup uncooked quick oats
1 cup golden raisins
½ cup (2 ounces) chopped mixed dried fruit
¼ cup (1 ounce) sunflower kernels
2 tablespoons butter
2 tablespoons packed light brown sugar
1 tablespoon honey
¼ teaspoon ground cinnamon
¼ teaspoon ground nutmeg

1. Preheat oven to 350°F. Spread oats on ungreased baking sheet; bake 10 to 15 minutes or until lightly toasted, stirring occasionally.

2. Combine popcorn, oats, raisins, dried fruit and sunflower kernels in large bowl. Heat butter, sugar, honey, cinnamon and nutmeg in small saucepan over medium heat until butter is melted. Drizzle over popcorn mixture; toss to coat.   *Makes about 8 cups*

ortega® snack mix

3 cups lightly salted peanuts
3 cups corn chips
3 cups spoon-size shredded wheat cereal
2 cups lightly salted pretzels
1 package (1.25 ounces) ORTEGA® Taco Seasoning Mix
¼ cup (½ stick) butter or margarine, melted

COMBINE peanuts, corn chips, shredded wheat, pretzels, seasoning mix and butter in large bowl; toss well to coat. Store in airtight container or zipper-type plastic bag.   *Makes about 20 servings*

Tip: Think ORTEGA Snack Mix the next time you need a hostess gift or something special for a teacher or friend. It tosses together in minutes and is always a hit. Place the mix in a cellophane bag tied with a ribbon with the recipe card attached. Or, consider packaging it in a decorative tin.

popcorn granola

acknowledgments

The publisher would like to thank the companies and organizations listed below for the use of their recipes and photographs in this publication.

ACH Food Companies, Inc.

Alouette® Cheese, Chavrie® Cheese, Saladena®, Montrachet®

Bob Evans®

Cabot® Creamery Cooperative

Del Monte Corporation

Dole Food Company, Inc.

Florida Department of Agriculture and Consumer Services, Bureau of Seafood and Aquaculture

The Hershey Company

Hormel Foods, LLC

JOLLY TIME® Pop Corn

McIlhenny Company (TABASCO® brand Pepper Sauce)

National Pork Board

National Turkey Federation

Ortega®, A Division of B&G Foods, Inc.

Reckitt Benckiser Inc.

StarKist® Tuna

Sun•Maid® Growers of California

Unilever

Wisconsin Milk Marketing Board

A

Alouette® Crème de Brie® Appetizers
with Caramelized Onion, 92
Apple Salsa with Cilantro and Lime,
4
Artichoke Hearts
Artichoke Crostini, 48
Crab and Artichoke Stuffed
Mushrooms, 90
Hot Artichoke Dip, 10
Marinated Antipasto, 88
Marinated Artichoke Cheese Toasts, 92
Spinach-Artichoke Party Cups, 98
Tex-Mex Artichoke Dip, 18
Tuna Artichoke Cups, 40
Asparagus & Prosciutto Antipasto, 102
Avocado
Fast Guacamole and "Chips," 18
Ortega® Green Chile Guacamole, 8
Santa Fe Shrimp Martini Cocktails, 94

B

Bacon
Bacon-Wrapped Breadsticks, 62
BLT Dip, 6
Individual Spinach & Bacon Quiches,
82
Nutty Bacon Cheeseball, 16
Oysters Romano, 96
Pineapple-Scallop Bites, 84
Sausage-Bacon-Apricot Kabobs, 50
Tex-Mex Potato Skins, 66
Baked Brie, 100
Barbecue Pizza, 58
Basil'd Cream Cheese with Capers, 102
Beans
Mini Chickpea Cakes, 26
Onion & White Bean Spread, 10
Ortega® Nachos, 38
Quick & Easy Hummus, 8
Refried Bean and Cheese Quesadillas,
70
Triangle Tostadas, 46
Tuscan White Bean Crostini, 44
Beef
Beef Pinwheels, 56
Mini Marinated Beef Skewers, 70
Reuben Dip, 22
Roast Beef Roll-Ups, 34
Texas Pecan and Beef Dip, 12

Beer and Coconut-Macadamia Shrimp,
86
BLT Dip, 6
Bruschetta & Crostini
Artichoke Crostini, 48
Grilled Summer Bruschetta, 24
Tomato and Caper Crostini, 30
Tuscan White Bean Crostini, 44
Two Tomato-Kalamata Crostini,
41
Bubbling Wisconsin Cheese Bread,
32

C

Cajun Deviled Eggs, 42
Cajun Wings, 76
Cheese Chile Dip, 14
Cheesy Chips, 112
Cheesy Christmas Trees, 88
Chicken
Barbecue Pizza, 58
Cajun Wings, 76
Chipotle Chicken Quesadillas, 68
Original Buffalo Chicken Wings,
76
Santa Fe Wings, 76
Snappy Chicken Wings, 56
Chile 'n' Cheese Spirals, 28
Chili Dip, 14
Chili Puffs, 36
Chipotle Chicken Quesadillas, 68
Chipotle Chile-Sour Cream Dip, 15
Chocolate
Chocolate & Fruit Snack Mix,
117
Crunchy-Fruity Snack Mix, 110
Everything but the Kitchen Sink,
118
Peanut Butter 'n' Chocolate Chips
Snack Mix, 120
Sweet Nothings Trail Mix, 117
Teddy Bear Party Mix, 112
Crab and Artichoke Stuffed Mushrooms,
90
Crab Cakes with Horseradish Mustard
Sauce, 97
Cranberries
Crunchy-Fruity Snack Mix, 110
Glitterrazzi Pop Corn, 110
Teddy Bear Party Mix, 112

E
Easiest Three-Cheese Fondue, 6
Easy Sausage Empanadas, 60
Easy Spinach Appetizer, 74
Everything but the Kitchen Sink, 118

F
Fast Guacamole and "Chips," 18
Fast Pesto Focaccia, 28
Fiesta Dip, 20
French-Style Pizza Bites, 78

G
Glitterrazzi Pop Corn, 110
Grilled Summer Bruschetta, 24

H
Ham
  Ham and Cherry Roll-Ups, 78
  Honey Roasted Ham Biscuits, 38
Herb Cheese Twists, 48
Honey Crunch Popcorn, 118
Honey Roasted Ham Biscuits, 38
Hot Artichoke Dip, 10
Hot Crab-Cheddar Spread, 15
Hot Pepper Cranberry Jelly Appetizer,
  106

I
Individual Spinach & Bacon Quiches,
  82

K
Kabobs
  Mini Marinated Beef Skewers, 70
  Pineapple-Scallop Bites, 84
  Sausage-Bacon-Apricot Kabobs, 50
  Tortellini Kabobs with Pesto Ranch
    Dip, 36

M
Margherita Panini Bites, 54
Marinated Antipasto, 88
Marinated Artichoke Cheese Toasts,
  92
Mediterranean Dip, 16
Micro Mini Stuffed Potatoes, 80
Mini Chickpea Cakes, 26
Mini Marinated Beef Skewers, 70
Mini Sausage Quiches, 73

Mushrooms
  Crab and Artichoke Stuffed
    Mushrooms, 90
  Pizza-Stuffed Mushrooms, 72
  Sausage-Stuffed Mushrooms, 32

N
Nuts (*see also* **Pecans**)
  Beer and Coconut-Macadamia Shrimp,
    86
  Chocolate & Fruit Snack Mix,
    117
  Crunchy-Fruity Snack Mix, 110
  Everything but the Kitchen Sink,
    118
  Glitterrazzi Pop Corn, 110
  Ham and Cherry Roll-Ups, 78
  Honey Roasted Ham Biscuits, 38
  Nutty Bacon Cheeseball, 16
  Nutty Onion Snack Mix, 116
  Ortega® Snack Mix, 122
  Super Bowl Snack Mix, 108
  Sweet Nothings Trail Mix, 117

O
Olives
  Beef Pinwheels, 56
  Chile 'n' Cheese Spirals, 28
  French-Style Pizza Bites, 78
  Marinated Antipasto, 88
  Olive & Feta Dip, 12
  Olive Tapenade, 22
  Tuna in Crispy Wonton Cups, 104
  Two Tomato-Kalamata Crostini,
    41
Onion & White Bean Spread, 10
Original Buffalo Chicken Wings, 76
Ortega® Green Chile Guacamole, 8
Ortega® Nachos, 38
Ortega® Snack Mix, 122
Oysters Romano, 96

P
Peanut Butter
  Peanut Butter 'n' Chocolate Chips
    Snack Mix, 120
  Peanut Butter Peanut Caramel
    Popcorn, 114
  Summer Fruits with Peanut
    Butter-Honey Dip, 26

Pecans
  Baked Brie, 100
  Honey Crunch Popcorn, 118
  Nutty Bacon Cheeseball, 16
  Sweet & Spicy Beer Nuts, 120
  Texas Pecan and Beef Dip, 12
Pepperoni
  Barbecue Pizza, 58
  Pizza-Stuffed Mushrooms, 72
  Stromboli Sticks, 42
Pineapple
  Crunchy-Fruity Snack Mix, 110
  Pineapple-Mango Salsa, 20
  Pineapple-Scallop Bites, 84
Pizza
  Barbecue Pizza, 58
  French-Style Pizza Bites, 78
  Polenta Pizzas, 34
Pizza-Stuffed Mushrooms, 72
Pork
  Pork Tenderloin Sliders, 64
  Triangle Tostadas, 46

Q
Quick & Easy Hummus, 8

R
Refried Bean and Cheese Quesadillas, 70
Reuben Dip, 22
Roast Beef Roll-Ups, 34

S
Salmon Appetizers, 100
Santa Fe Shrimp Martini Cocktails, 94
Santa Fe Wings, 76
Sausage
  Easy Sausage Empanadas, 60
  Mini Sausage Quiches, 73
  Polenta Pizzas, 34
  Sausage-Bacon-Apricot Kabobs, 50
  Sausage-Stuffed Mushrooms, 32
  Spicy Mustard Kielbasa Bites, 62
Seafood (see also **Tuna**)
  Beer and Coconut-Macadamia Shrimp, 86
  Crab and Artichoke Stuffed Mushrooms, 90
  Crab Cakes with Horseradish Mustard Sauce, 97

Seafood (continued)
  Hot Crab-Cheddar Spread, 15
  Oysters Romano, 96
  Pineapple-Scallop Bites, 84
  Salmon Appetizers, 100
  Santa Fe Shrimp Martini Cocktails, 94
  Smoked Salmon Roses, 90
  Spicy Marinated Shrimp, 106
Snappy Chicken Wings, 56
Spanish Tapas Potatoes, 52
Spicy Marinated Shrimp, 106
Spicy Mustard Kielbasa Bites, 62
Spicy Turkey Ham Spread, 14
Spinach
  Easy Spinach Appetizer, 74
  Individual Spinach & Bacon Quiches, 82
  Spinach-Artichoke Party Cups, 98
Stromboli Sticks, 42
Summer Fruits with Peanut Butter-Honey Dip, 26
Super Bowl Snack Mix, 108
Sweet & Spicy Beer Nuts, 120
Sweet Nothings Trail Mix, 117

T
Taco Popcorn Olé, 114
Teddy Bear Party Mix, 112
Texas Pecan and Beef Dip, 12
Tex-Mex Artichoke Dip, 18
Tex-Mex Potato Skins, 66
Tomato and Caper Crostini, 30
Tortellini Kabobs with Pesto Ranch Dip, 36
Triangle Tostadas, 46
Tuna
  Tuna Artichoke Cups, 40
  Tuna Focaccia Melt, 72
  Tuna in Crispy Wonton Cups, 104
Turkey: Spicy Turkey Ham Spread, 14
Tuscan White Bean Crostini, 44
Two Tomato-Kalamata Crostini, 41

W
Wisconsin Swiss Fondue, 96

Z
Zesty Blue Cheese Dip, 76
Zesty Buffalo Style Popcorn, 116

metric conversion chart

VOLUME MEASUREMENTS (dry)

1/8 teaspoon = 0.5 mL
1/4 teaspoon = 1 mL
1/2 teaspoon = 2 mL
3/4 teaspoon = 4 mL
1 teaspoon = 5 mL
1 tablespoon = 15 mL
2 tablespoons = 30 mL
1/4 cup = 60 mL
1/3 cup = 75 mL
1/2 cup = 125 mL
2/3 cup = 150 mL
3/4 cup = 175 mL
1 cup = 250 mL
2 cups = 1 pint = 500 mL
3 cups = 750 mL
4 cups = 1 quart = 1 L

VOLUME MEASUREMENTS (fluid)

1 fluid ounce (2 tablespoons) = 30 mL
4 fluid ounces (1/2 cup) = 125 mL
8 fluid ounces (1 cup) = 250 mL
12 fluid ounces (1 1/2 cups) = 375 mL
16 fluid ounces (2 cups) = 500 mL

WEIGHTS (mass)

1/2 ounce = 15 g
1 ounce = 30 g
3 ounces = 90 g
4 ounces = 120 g
8 ounces = 225 g
10 ounces = 285 g
12 ounces = 360 g
16 ounces = 1 pound = 450 g

DIMENSIONS

1/16 inch = 2 mm
1/8 inch = 3 mm
1/4 inch = 6 mm
1/2 inch = 1.5 cm
3/4 inch = 2 cm
1 inch = 2.5 cm

OVEN TEMPERATURES

250°F = 120°C
275°F = 140°C
300°F = 150°C
325°F = 160°C
350°F = 180°C
375°F = 190°C
400°F = 200°C
425°F = 220°C
450°F = 230°C

BAKING PAN SIZES

Utensil	Size in Inches/Quarts	Metric Volume	Size in Centimeters
Baking or Cake Pan (square or rectangular)	8×8×2	2 L	20×20×5
	9×9×2	2.5 L	23×23×5
	12×8×2	3 L	30×20×5
	13×9×2	3.5 L	33×23×5
Loaf Pan	8×4×3	1.5 L	20×10×7
	9×5×3	2 L	23×13×7
Round Layer Cake Pan	8×1½	1.2 L	20×4
	9×1½	1.5 L	23×4
Pie Plate	8×1¼	750 mL	20×3
	9×1¼	1 L	23×3
Baking Dish or Casserole	1 quart	1 L	—
	1½ quart	1.5 L	—
	2 quart	2 L	—